ST

D0388415

This is the b

You wouldn't want to spoil a great ending!

This book is printed "manga-style," in the authentic Japanese right-to-left format. Since none of the artwork has been flipped or altered, readers get to experience the story just as the creator intended. You've been asking for it, so TOKYOPOP® delivered: authentic, hot-off-the-press, and far more fun!

DIRECTIONS

If this is your first time reading manga-style, here's a quick guide to help you understand how it works.

It's easy... just start in the top right panel and follow the numbers. Have fun, and look for more 100% authentic manga from TOKYOPOP®!

FOR MORE INFORMATION VISIT: WWW.TOKYOPOP.COM

SUPER HYPER AUDIOTISTIC SONIC REVOLUTION!!!

www.myspace.com/tokyopop

www.TOKYOPOP.com

Available at the iTunes Music Store and everywhere music downloads are available. Keyword: TOKYOPOP

New releases every month! Check out these great albums AVAILABLE NOW!!!

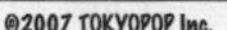
©2007 TOKYOPOP Inc.

TOKYOPOP MANGA SUPPLEMENT

ELEMENTAL GELADE
6
An action-packed otaku favorite!
Rowen and Kuea battle Grayarts on the deck of a cruise ship...but can they defeat him before they all get that "sinking" feeling? Later, Coud tries to sneak into the country to avoid trouble at customs...but is this such a good idea when there are assassins hot on his tail?
The inspiration for the popular anime available from Geneon
ACTION
T
TEEN AGE 13+
© MAYUMI AZUMA/MAG Garden

FOR MORE INFORMATION VISIT: WWW.TOKYOPOP.COM

HARUKAZE BITTER★BOP™
WELCOME TO THE SCHOOL OF HARD KNOCKS!
BB

School delinquent Chiyoharu's turned over a new leaf, but the appearance of one amnesiac superhuman and one ditzy self-proclaimed detective isn't about to make his life any easier.

COMEDY

T TEEN AGE 13+

© COURT BETTEN / MAG Garden

FOR MORE INFORMATION VISIT: WWW.TOKYOPOP.COM

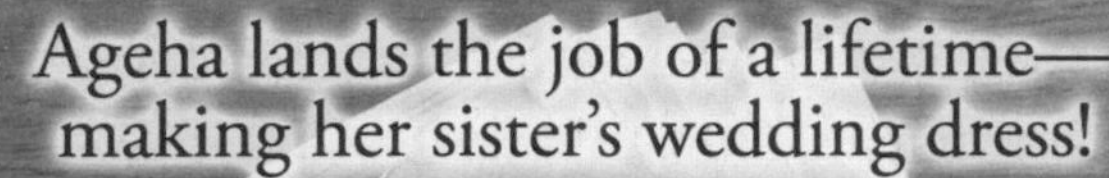

Ageha lands the job of a lifetime—making her sister's wedding dress!

From the creator of
I Hate You More Than Anyone!
and
Tears of a Lamb

Pure shojo bliss full of weddings, frills...and romance!

Despite being shocked and heartbroken by her sister's upcoming marriage to the most boring man alive, Ageha quickly jumps in to help when the wedding dressmaker hurts his hand! Thus begin her adventures working at Velvet Blue Rose, the super-exclusive bridal-design shop run by two super-hot guys!

© Banri Hidaka

FOR MORE INFORMATION VISIT: WWW.TOKYOPOP.COM

TOKYOPOP MANGA SUPPLEMENT

THE CONTINUING ADVENTURES OF THE LITTLE VAMPIRE WHO COULDN'T!

chibi Vampire™ 7

INSPIRED THE *KARIN* ANIME!

When Kenta discovers why Karin's blood increases around him, their relationship shatters, and they struggle to deal with the thought of losing each other. Is there light at the end of the tunnel? And what secrets in the past explain Kenta's hatred of his father? Will the two of them finally make up and bring happiness to the whole family?

© Yuna Kagesaki

FOR MORE INFORMATION VISIT: WWW.TOKYOPOP.COM

.hack//G.U.+™

"The World" as it's never been seen before!

In the three years since the events of *.hack//Legend of the Twilight,* The World has become The World R:2...a dangerous game overrun by player killers and where lawlessness abounds. Follow Haseo as he chases Tri-Edge and gets involved with Project G.U. and the mysterious AIDA that plague The World R:2!

© 2006 .hack Conglomerate © NBGI / KADOKAWA SHOTEN

FOR MORE INFORMATION VISIT: WWW.TOKYOPOP.COM

+ANIMA
7
The extraordinary adventures of the +Anima continue...
Cooro and his fellow +Anima companions travel through the darkest of passages toward the city of Sailand—a place where unbeknownst to them, +Anima are kept as slaves! As they arrive to town, slave traders capture Husky and Senri, and it's up to Cooro and Nana to free them. But can Cooro and Nana stage a jailbreak without being captured themselves? Find out in +Anima Volume 7!
+ANIMA
TOKYOPOP
7
Natsumi Mukai
FANTASY
T
TEEN AGE 13+
© Mukai Natsumi/Media Works
"An enjoyable romp for comic readers with a sweet tooth."
—Publishers Weekly

FOR MORE INFORMATION VISIT: WWW.TOKYOPOP.COM

TOKYOPOP MANGA SUPPLEMENT

Fruits Basket™

By Natsuki Takaya

Volume 19

Can Tohru free Kyo of his curse?

Tohru is conflicted as she realizes she might love Kyo more than she loves her mom. Then Shigure shows up to let her know that all the members of the Zodiac look down on Kyo. If she wants to save Kyo, she'll have to break his curse first!

Winner of the American Anime Award for Best Manga!

The #1 selling shojo manga in America!

ROMANCE

T
TEEN AGE 13+

© 1998 Natsuki Takaya / HAKUSENSHA, Inc.

FOR MORE INFORMATION VISIT: WWW.TOKYOPOP.COM

GAKUEN ALICE VOLUME TWO
Mikan is officially accepted into the mysterious Alice Academy, but things aren't exactly going smoothly...
Mikan is off to a rough start! Natsume still bullies her, her class ranking couldn't be lower, some of the teachers are outright hostile and she has been forbidden to contact anyone outside of the school. Will she be able to find others like her at the Academy, or will she be betrayed by the only people she still trusts?
The hit series from Japan CONTINUES!
Gakuen ALICE
TACHIBANA HIGUCHI
2
TOKYOPOP
FANTASY
T
TEEN AGE 13+
© 2003 Tachibana Higuchi / HAKUSENSHA, Inc.

FOR MORE INFORMATION VISIT: WWW.TOKYOPOP.COM

TOKYOPOP MANGA SUPPLEMENT

An anthology with new stories and art by

TOKYOPOP's top talent!

Princess Ai: Rumors from the Other Side

Who would dare print trashy rumors, innuendo and bold-faced lies about international rock diva Princess Ai? TOKYOPOP would! Ai is an outspoken, outrageous, controversial celebrity, so it wasn't hard to find incredible stories from people who love her, hate her and love to hate her. Brought to you by Misaho Kujiradou and TOKYOPOP's top talent, these 12 all-new, spurious stories take a totally twisted view of Princess Ai and her friends. This counterfactual collection also includes a sneak peek at the new Princess Ai trilogy drawn by the fabulous Misaho Kujiradou!

Includes a sneak peek at the upcoming manga trilogy!

© & TM TOKYOPOP, Inc. and Kitty Radio, Inc.

FOR MORE INFORMATION VISIT: WWW.TOKYOPOP.COM

April 18-20, 2008

at the Jacob Javits Center, New York City

New York Comic Con is Coming!

Find the best in **Anime, Manga, Graphic Novels, Video Games, Toys, and Movies!** NY Comic Con has hundreds of **Celebrity Appearances, Autographing Sessions, Screenings, Industry Panels, Gaming Tournaments, and Much More!**

Go to **www.nycomiccon.com** to get all the information and **BUY TICKETS!** Plus, sign up for special New York Comic Con updates to be the first to learn about Guests, Premieres, and Special Events!

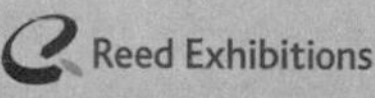

TOKYOPOP MANGA SUPPLEMENT

BASED ON THE BEST-SELLING MANGA AND ANIME!

Naota's life couldn't be more complicated...or could it?

FLCL™
THE NOVEL 1

Naota lives with his eccentric father and grandfather; his brother's ex-girlfriend constantly makes passes at him; and to top it off, an impish, playful alien has just run over him with her Vespa! Little does he know that this is only the beginning of his involvement in an interplanetary, ideological war.

© 1999 GAINAX ©Yoji ENOKIDO 2000 / KADOKAWA SHOTEN Publishing

FOR MORE INFORMATION VISIT: WWW.TOKYOPOP.COM

TOKYOPOP MANGA SUPPLEMENT

THE SPECTACULAR FANTASY EPIC CONTINUES!

THE TWELVE KINGDOMS™

SEA OF WIND

"A compelling translation that sucks you into the story and won't let go."
-Newtype USA

Taiki must learn to accept not only that he is a unicorn—and not human!—but that he is also in charge of choosing and protecting the king of Tai. He is visited by various men and women, all hoping to be selected as king. With little guidance (and no knowledge of how to transform into unicorn form), he must choose a king... Will he make the right choice?

INSPIRED THE ANIME!

POP FICTION

© Fuyumi Ono / KODANSHA LTD.

FOR MORE INFORMATION VISIT: WWW.TOKYOPOP.COM

TOKYOPOP®.com

WHERE MANGA LIVES!

JOIN the TOKYOPOP community:
www.TOKYOPOP.com

COME AND PREVIEW THE HOTTEST MANGA AROUND!

CREATE...
UPLOAD...
DOWNLOAD...
BLOG...
CHAT...
VOTE...
LIVE!!!!

WWW.TOKYOPOP.COM HAS:

- Exclusives
- News
- Contests
- Games
- Rising Stars of Manga
- iManga
- and more...

TOKYOPOP.COM 2.0 NOW LIVE!

© & TM TOKYOPOP Inc. and Kitty Radio, Inc.

Psychic Power Nanaki Vol. 2

Created by Ryo Saenagi

Translation - Elina Ishikawa
English Adaptation - Alex de Campi
Retouch and Lettering - Star Print Brokers
Production Artist - Michael Paolilli
Graphic Designer - James Lee

Editor - Peter Ahlstrom
Digital Imaging Manager - Chris Buford
Pre-Production Supervisor - Erika Terriquez
Production Manager - Elisabeth Brizzi
Managing Editor - Vy Nguyen
Art Director - Anne Marie Horne
Editor-in-Chief - Rob Tokar
Publisher - Mike Kiley
President and C.O.O. - John Parker
C.E.O. and Chief Creative Officer - Stuart Levy

TOKYOPOP and are trademarks or registered trademarks of TOKYOPOP Inc.

TOKYOPOP Inc.
5900 Wilshire Blvd. Suite 2000
Los Angeles, CA 90036

E-mail: info@TOKYOPOP.com
Come visit us online at www.TOKYOPOP.com

CHOU SHINRIGENSHOU NOURYOKUSHA NANAKI by Ryo Saenagi © 2004 Ryo Saenagi All rights reserved. First published in Japan in 2004 by HAKUSENSHA, INC., Tokyo English language translation rights in the United States of America and Canada arranged with HAKUSENSHA, INC., Tokyo through Tuttle-Mori Agency Inc., Tokyo English text copyright © 2008 TOKYOPOP Inc.

All rights reserved. No portion of this book may be reproduced or transmitted in any form or by any means without written permission from the copyright holders. This manga is a work of fiction. Any resemblance to actual events or locales or persons, living or dead, is entirely coincidental.

ISBN: 978-1-4278-0305-4

First TOKYOPOP printing: March 2008

10 9 8 7 6 5 4 3 2 1

Printed in the USA

PSYCHIC POWER NANAKI™

If the Shoe fits, Wear it.

Volume 2

by
Ryo Saenagi

HAMBURG // LONDON // LOS ANGELES // TOKYO

CONTENTS

CHRONICLE 7 6
CHRONICLE 8 39
CHRONICLE 9 69
CHRONICLE 10 99
CHRONICLE 11 129
CHRONICLE 12 159
I CAN DO IT MYSELF 189
POSTSCRIPT 191

THE STORY SO FAR...

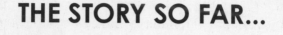

When an auto accident awakens a mysterious power within high school teen Shunsuke Nanaki, he discovers he's a psychic! The Paranormal Task Force, the LOCK Agency, recruits him to help solve supernatural mysteries and pairs him up with the young-looking Ao Kudo. Ao is at first reluctant to work with the brash and reckless teenager, but Nanaki's creativity and resourcefulness during a couple tough cases convince Ao he's not so bad. However, Nanaki soon learns of the dangers and temptations facing a psychic—it's all too easy to get drunk on the power and turn into a "freak"... something which apparently happened to Ao's former partner, who has disappeared...

PSYCHIC POWER
NANAKI™
CHRONICLE 7

LOCK

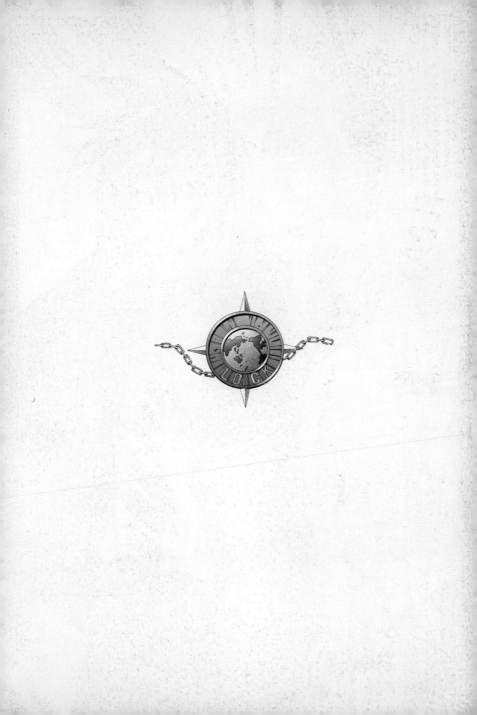

SFF
FLOAT

HA HA HA.
WOBBLE
WOBBLE
CHECK MY SKILLS, OLD MAN!
I SEE. NOW TRY TO TELEPORT IT.
PIECE OF CAKE.
HERE.
POOF!
HUH?
WHERE'D THIS WHITE POWDER COME FROM?
Crap, it's all over my jacket!
FROM THE OBJECT. YOU BLEW IT INTO SMITHEREENS.
WE WON'T BE LETTING YOU TACKLE TELEPORTATION LEVEL TWO ANYTIME SOON, THEN.
WHAT WAS LEVEL TWO AGAIN?

THE TELEPORTATION OF ORGANIC MATTER.
PLANTS, SMALL ANIMALS...
THEY'RE QUITE HARD TO WASH OFF YOUR JACKET WHEN YOU MESS UP.
I DON'T MESS UP IN REAL LIFE. I TELEPORT MYSELF ALL THE TIME!
THAT'S A SURPRISE.
GIVE ME A BREAK. I'VE ALWAYS HATED TAKING TESTS.
BESIDES, IF YOUR TESTS WERE MORE INTERESTING, I'D WORK HARDER.
WHAT DO YOU MEAN, "MORE INTERESTING"?
TELEPORTING MONEY OUT OF BANK VAULTS, NOW *THAT'S* A TEST I COULD GET BEHIND!
TRY THAT, AND *I'LL* BLOW *YOU* INTO SMITHEREENS.

BE HERE FOR TRAINING BEFORE SCHOOL TOMORROW.
AND MAKE AN EFFORT, FOR ONCE.
WHAT-EVER.

MAN, I HATE DOING LAPS.

IT'S SO POINTLESS. GYM SUCKS.

LESS TALKING! MORE RUNNING!

WHOOOSH

BWA HA HA HA HA!

HOLD IT RIGHT THERE, NANAKI!
おらあっ
WHAT'D I DO?
NO SKATE-BOARDING OR ROLLERBLADING ON THE RUNNING TRACK!
HEY, NANAKI. LET ME HAVE A GO!
SURE. 100 YEN PER LAP.
DO YOU WANT TO DO EXTRA LAPS AFTER SCHOOL?
Hell no!
CHILL OUT. I'LL PUT IT AWAY.

THAT GIRL...
I'VE NEVER SEEN HER BEFORE.
Who is she?
SHE'S STARING AT ME.
She's kinda hot.
UEJIN, WHO'S THAT?
WHO?
WHERE?
What?!
SHE'S GONE!

MAN, MY FEET ARE KILLING ME.

I'm starving.

LET'S HAVE LUNCH.

I'M GONNA GRAB SOMETHING AT THE STORE. I'LL CATCH YOU LATER.

OKAY.

And so, like, four million people saw.

Hah. Serves him right.

NA-NAKI, RIGHT?

YOU'RE THAT GIRL...

LET'S HAVE LUNCH TOGETHER.
I'M TAKEKO KITAMI IN CLASS 1-C.
TAKEKO, HUH?
SO WHAT DO YOU WANT FROM ME?
MAYBE I JUST WANT TO HAVE LUNCH WITH YOU.
!
NA-NAAAKI ...
YEAH?
LITTLE FRESHMAN'S GOT A CRUSH ON NANAKI!
AO, YOU ←(?) SO WISH YOU WERE ME.

Hi! I'm Ryo Saenagi!!!
Here's Nanaki volume two! Thank God.
So what should I do with my column? Hmm. I guess I'll talk about this manga for a change.
And I'd also like to mention something that bothered me a little in the fan letters I received.
See you later...
Pant
CAN YOU FLOAT IN THE AIR?
Pant
WHAT ?!

SO, DO YOU TELEPORT TO SCHOOL INSTANTLY?

DO YOU KNOW WINNING LOTTERY NUMBERS AHEAD OF TIME?

DO YOU USE CLAIRVOYANCE TO SPY ON THE GIRLS' LOCKER ROOM?

What?!

YOU NEVER USED THESE CARDS BEFORE?!

SHOW ME YOUR SKILLS WITH THESE ZENER CARDS!

JUST TELL ME WHAT THEY ARE.

What are Zener cards?
THEY'RE E.S.P. CARDS! THEY TEST YOUR E.S.P.!
I KNOW YOU'RE A PSYCHIC!
WHA--
E.S.P. cards?!

YOU WERE LATE TO SCHOOL YESTERDAY.
ME TOO. I OVERSLEPT.
Oh no, they must be taking attendance now.
CRAP!
I FORGOT MY CELL PHONE!
LET'S SEE... WHERE WAS IT... OH YEAH, NEXT TO MY BED.
POOF!
!!
WHAAAT?!
TEE HEE. ♡ I SAW YOU DO IT.

IT WAS LIKE WATCHING A UFO APPEAR! OR SEEING A FAERIE!
ほう…
Oh!
I HAVEN'T SEEN ANY FAERIES, BUT I KNOW THEY EXIST.
SHE--
SHE'S AN OCCULT FREAK!

What a pain.

I GOTTA DEAL WITH THIS **FAST**.

HEY, TAKEKO.

YES?

THAT BRAT AO WILL NEVER SHUT UP IF HE FINDS OUT I USED MY POWER OUTSIDE OF WORK.

You fool...

I HATE TO BREAK IT TO YOU, BUT WHAT YOU SAW WAS JUST SLEIGHT OF HAND.

たす。

WHAT? BUT I'M *SURE* I SAW...
I KNOW YOU *WANT* TO BELIEVE IN E.S.P...
DO YOU REALLY THINK IF I HAD E.S.P...
...I'D BE GOING TO THIS DUMP OF A SCHOOL?
Common Sense
BUT...
FOR STARTERS...
BUT...
THANKS FOR LUNCH.
If you don't want to weird guys out, lay off the occult stuff.

I GUESS I'LL JUST HAVE TO PROVE I'M RIGHT.
SLAM
...JEEZ.
スタスタ

Faculty Room
Hey!
PERFECT TIMING, NANAKI.
CAN YOU HELP ME CARRY SOME THINGS TO GEOGRAPHY CLASS?
UM, NOT REALLY...
PLEEEASE, NAAANAKI!!
OKAY, FINE.
If you'll stop begging...
Li'l
Li'l
Li'l mustache no way!
NAAA-NAKI! ♡
!!

MY, YOU SURE ARE JUMPY!

I FORGOT TO GIVE YOU A PRESENT EARLIER. CATCH!

ポーンッ

!!!

...WHAT THE HELL DID YOU DO THAT FOR?!

I MADE IT SPECIALLY FOR YOU.

WEIRDEST. GIRL. EVER.

CLICK

!!

HIM? OF COURSE HE'S ALL RIGHT.

!

SHE'S TRYING TO TRICK ME INTO USING MY POWER.

She even brought a camcorder.

A GIRL NAMED TAKEKO KITAMI. SHE'S A FRESHMAN.

REALLY? COOL.

NANAKI, LET'S WALK HOME TOGETHER!

OH.

YOU OKAY, NANAKI?

She's ba-ack...

GO...

...AWAY!

WHAT?
UGH.
WHY?!
YOU'RE SUCH A MEANIE!
ball

WHOA! YOU OKAY, NANAKI?
I THINK HE'S STOPPED BREATHING.
Ack!

DO SOMETHING... ABOUT THAT GIRL...
Uh...
NO THANKS. I GOT ENOUGH BRUISES AS IT IS.
Wuss!
WHAT AM I GONNA DO?
HANG ON, I GOT A WAY TO GET RID OF HER!
FIND HER A BOYFRIEND!
Mind your own business.
What?!
Stay away from our boys, freshman.
THAT'S GENIUS!

NANAKI! GOOD MORNING!

THERE YOU ARE, BACK LIKE A BAD SMELL.

YOU BETTER BE READY TODAY!

YOU DON'T KNOW WHEN TO GIVE UP.
I TOLD YOU, IT WAS SLEIGHT OF HAND.
IT'S OKAY, NANAKI! YOU CAN ADMIT YOUR POWERS TO ME!
POOF
I WON'T SELL YOUR STORY TO THE TABLOIDS.
RUSTLE
EEEEP!
A BUG!
PLOP
たし。
Gasp!

A BABY DRAGON! ♡
I always knew they existed!
GOTCHA !!
GRIP

Who do you think you are?

IT'S GONE!
THAT WAS AMAZING ...
I'M IMPRESSED.
BUT NO ONE WILL BELIEVE ME WITHOUT PROOF...
CRAP...
OH YEAH! YOU SAW IT TOO...
... NANAKIII!
CRAP! IT BACK-FIRED!

HEY.
!
AO!

WHUMP!

WHAT'S UP?

SOME JERK SKIPPED HIS TRAINING YESTERDAY, SO I'VE BEEN ORDERED TO WARN HIM.

...YOU BRAT.

AND I FOUND THIS, FALLING OUT OF THE SKY.

!!

UM, PARDON ME.

I'M BUSY RIGHT NOW!

Go look for faeries or something.

?

WHAT KIND OF GIRL IS YOUR TYPE?!
HUH?

? WHO-- ?
HEY, WAIT A MINUTE...
I'M TAKEKO KITAMI IN CLASS 1-C.
WHAT'S YOUR NAME?
Nanaki

WHEN'S YOUR BIRTHDAY?
WHO CARES?
WHAT'S YOUR BLOOD TYPE?
WHO CARES?
ANY HOBBIES?
...I SAID, WHO CARES?
ANOTHER GIRL FALLS FOR HIS GOOD LOOKS...
What a joke!
ふっ...
Hmph!
C'mon!
THAT'S NOT AN ANSWER! ♡

DON'T TURN A BLIND EYE TO THE TRUTH.
IT'S NOT HARD TO GUESS WHERE YOU BELONG.

PSYCHIC POWER
NANAKI™
CHRONICLE 8

MURDER?!

BLIP
BUT DIDN'T THE POLICE SAY IT WAS AN ACCI-DENT?
WE DON'T KNOW THAT YET.
BUT THERE ARE ENOUGH DISTURBING ASPECTS TO THE CASE THAT THEY'VE ASKED LOCK TO INVESTI-GATE.

LOCK

Anything could happen.

THE VICTIMS WERE TWO FEMALES, FRIENDS FROM COLLEGE.
THE WOMAN ON THE RIGHT LOST CONTROL OF HER VEHICLE WHILE TALKING ON HER CELL PHONE.
Morita, Az

THE OTHER WOMAN SLIPPED AND FELL ON HER APARTMENT BUILDING'S STAIRS.
Manami

SO, ONE DEAD FROM STUPIDITY, THE OTHER FROM A BROKEN HEEL?
THE POLICE FOUND NO FOUL PLAY AT THE SCENES OR ON THE BODIES.

THEN WHY DO WE NEED TO INVESTI-GATE?

COMPUTER, SHOW THE NEXT FILE.

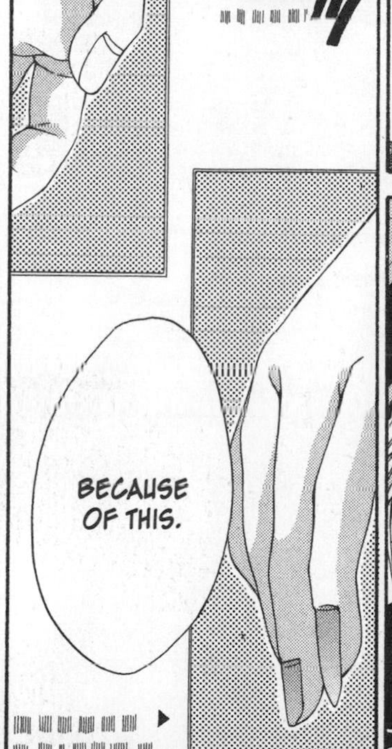
BECAUSE OF THIS.

FINGER-NAILS?
YES. THEY EACH HAD A FINGERNAIL CLIPPED SHORTLY BEFORE THEY DIED.
SOME SERIAL KILLERS KEEP THEIR VICTIMS' BELONGINGS OR BODY PARTS FOR MEMORABILIA.
SO THEY ALWAYS HAVE REMINDERS OF THEIR CRIMES CLOSE AT HAND.
A ME-MENTO?
HUH? WHAT DO YOU MEAN?
SINCE WHEN DO YOU KNOW ANYTHING ABOUT REAL COP STUFF?
I THOUGHT GHOSTS AND PSYCHICS WERE THE ONLY THINGS ON YOUR MIND!
WHY, YOU...
VMMM

EXCUSE US.

HI THERE!

HUH ?!

What're two pretty girls doing here?

WHO ARE THEY?

Oh?

YOU HAVEN'T MET THEM?

I KNOW YOU!! YOU'RE NANAKI-KUN!

I've seen your picture.

THAT CAREFREE ONE IS KANADE HONJO.

Hi hi!

THE INTENSE ONE IS SATSUKI KIRYU.

Who're you calling intense, Gunji-san?

THEY'RE THIRD-YEARS IN JUNIOR HIGH. AND THEY'RE LOCK MEMBERS.

What?

I THOUGHT THERE WERE JUST THREE OF US IN THIS DIVISION.

WHAT'S HER DEAL?

SHE KEEPS STARING AT ME.
LIKE I'VE DONE SOMETHING.

HEY, KANADE.

TAKE A LOOK AT THE VICTIMS' PERSONAL BELONGINGS.

'KAY.

WHAT'S SHE GONNA DO?

WAIT AND SEE.

Something in the fan letters has been bothering me. And it's that...

Ao is remarkably popular.

I was pretty surprised about this. He was originally planned to talk in a very polite manner, but changed completely in the storyboard for the first episode. If I had drawn him as planned, would he have been less popular? Hmm... He wasn't even supposed to get smart with Gunji, either... I guess you can't rely on the character sketch (lol). I mean, Ao naturally began talking like that all by himself! As I had mentioned in volume one, characters tend to go off in their own, unexpected directions. Another thing that bothered me was that...

Nanaki is abnormally unpopular.

I'm sorry, dude...but you know I love you (lol)!

AAAAAH!

?!

WANNA GO THERE NOW?

fortunetelling

fortune telling

NANAKI, DID YOU FIND ANYTHING?
NOPE. NONE OF THE FOR-TUNETELLERS RECOGNIZE THE VICTIMS.

HEY.
!
I'M SORRY, BUT PLEASE WAIT YOUR TURN.
......!!

WHY DID YOU COME BARGING IN HERE?
OH, WE'RE NOT HERE TO GET OUR FORTUNES TOLD.
HEY, AO, YOU EXPLAIN.
WHAT THE...?
I GOT MY READING, SO I'LL LEAVE.
Oh.
I'M SORRY ABOUT THIS.
Thank you.
PLEASE EXPLAIN YOURSELVES.
THANKS. THIS WON'T TAKE LONG.
SHUT

HAVE YOU EVER SEEN THESE TWO WOMEN?

WHY DON'T I DO A READING FOR YOU?
FOR FREE, AS A SAMPLE.
COOL! OKAY, ME FIRST!
THAT WAS FAST.
……
I'LL LOOK INTO WHAT CONCERNS YOU MOST. HOW'S THAT?
Sure.
WHAT-EVER.
THEN, PLEASE BE SILENT FOR A MOMENT.

HEY, AO, WHAT HAPPENS IN CRYSTAL BALLS?

CRYSTAL GAZING IS CLASSIFIED AS A KIND OF INTUITION.

THE CRYSTAL SHOWS MENTAL IMAGES OF THE PAST AND PRESENT, AS WELL AS FEARS AND IMPRESSIONS.

THERE'S A BIRD.

!

?!

WHAT ABOUT YOU?

NO THANKS.

WHY NOT, AO? IT'S FREE!

I like free.

SHUT UP.

LET GO OF ME.

ARE YOU SURE?

WHY ARE YOU STANDING THERE LIKE A SPAZ, AO?
......!!
SORRY. YOUR HAIR GOT CAUGHT IN MY BRACELET.
IT MUST BE A SIGN THAT YOU SHOULD HAVE YOUR FORTUNE READ.
EEP!

SLAM
OH MY.
Heh.
HE ESCAPED LIKE A LIZARD.
WHOA!
BRR! I'M FREEZING!

DID YOU JUST CALL ME?

NOPE.

...OKAY.

WHAT THE HELL?!

...WAS IT MY IMAGINATION?

I THOUGHT I HEARD SOMEONE CALL ME.

NGH.

KANADE'S TAKING A NAP HERE?

BUT WHERE'S GUNJI-SAN?

VMMM
YOU'RE BACK!
GUNJI-SAN HAD TO GO TO HEAD-QUARTERS.
YOU'RE STILL HERE TOO.

I WAS DOING SOME TRAIN-ING...
...AND WAITING FOR YOU.

WHY DID YOU TAKE SHUNSUKE NANAKI AS YOUR PARTNER?

SHUNSUKE NANAKI IS CALLOW AND IRRESPON-SIBLE.

HE CAN'T CONTROL HIMSELF. HOW MANY BUILDINGS HAS HE DESTROYED SO FAR?

How dare you?!

WELL, I CAN'T DENY THAT.

BUT HE'S STILL NEW TO LOCK.

Mistakes are to be expected.

I REFUSE TO ACCEPT HIM.

YOU ALREADY *HAVE* A PARTNER, AO!

I WILL NEVER FORGET.
YOU WERE SO KIND TO ME, HELPING ME NOT BE SCARED OF MY PSYCHIC ABILITIES.
I WORKED SO HARD ON MY TRAINING BECAUSE *I* WANTED TO BECOME YOUR PARTNER.
BUT I COULD NEVER BE BETTER THAN THE PARTNER YOU ALREADY HAD.
HE KNEW *EVERYTHING*. HE KNEW WHAT YOU WERE TRYING TO DO AHEAD OF TIME.
YOU COM-PLEMENTED EACH OTHER PERFECTLY...

...AND HE IS STILL YOUR *REAL* PARTNER!

YOU KNOW I'M RIGHT! THINK ABOUT IT!

ドス

ドス

SA-TSUKI!

DON'T IMAGINE HE WON'T COME BACK!

JERK!

KANADE, WE'RE GOING HOME!

Oof. I'm stuffed.

SLIDE

WAKE UP, LAZY-BONES!

ずるずるずる

.....

VMMM

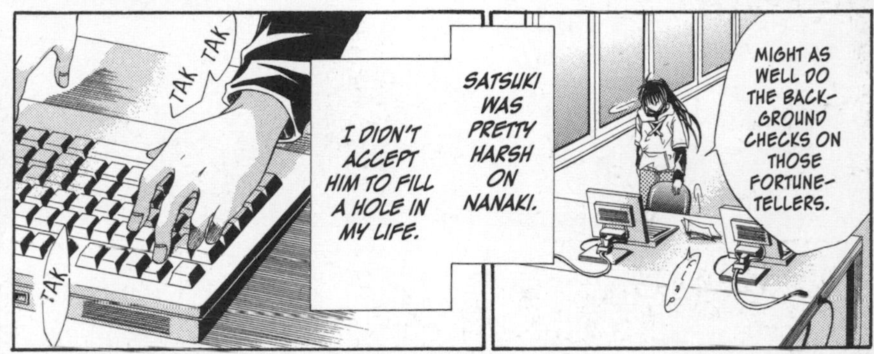

MIGHT AS WELL DO THE BACK-GROUND CHECKS ON THOSE FORTUNE-TELLERS.
SATSUKI WAS PRETTY HARSH ON NANAKI.
I DIDN'T ACCEPT HIM TO FILL A HOLE IN MY LIFE.
TAK TAK
TAK

Morihiro S

MORIHIRO SAI... THAT WAS THE LAST FORTUNE-TELLER.

...THE ONE WHO MENTIONED NANAKI'S NURSERY RHYME.

ALTHOUGH WHAT HE SAID WAS SO VAGUE IT COULD HAVE APPLIED TO--

!

WHAT THE...

COMPUTER, ACCESS THE LINKED CASE FILES.
ACCESS CODE REQUIRED.
AO KUDO, B-01.
CODE ACCEPTED. LOADING.
COMPUTER, OPEN FILE 0367528.
BLIP
ピクッ
COME HERE.
AO!
?!
It's the same voice that called to me outside the fortuneteller's shop.
THAT-- IN MY HEAD!
IS HE A TELEPATH?
LIKE NANAKI AND ME?
OR ARE WE JUST ON THE SAME PSYCHIC WAVE-LENGTH?

HOW ...
...DO YOU KNOW MY NAME?!
COME BACK!
YOUR REAL PARTNER IS WAITING FOR YOU.

GOING HOME? *NOW?!*

WHAT'S UP, NANAKI? YOU DITCHING US?

NO. I'VE JUST GOT... STUFF TO DEAL WITH.

DEAL WITH IT TOMORROW.

MY BOSS' NEW CHICK HATES HIS SILVER JEWELRY, SO HE'S GIVING IT TO US.

GUESS I SHOULD STAY!

GUESS YOU SHOULD!

Yeah! I love free stuff!

WELL, LOCK WON'T MIND IF I'M A LITTLE BIT LATE.

YO.

WHOA!
MAN, DO YOU EVER GIVE A GUY A BREAK?
YOU'RE LATE! WHERE HAVE YOU BEEN?

WE TRIED TO CALL, BUT YOUR CELL PHONE WAS TURNED OFF.
Uh-oh. Busted.
HEY, NANAKI-KUN!
AO-KUN DISAPPEARED!
...WHAT?
ARE YOU SERIOUS?
HE'S NOT HERE OR AT HEADQUARTERS, AND HE'S NOT ANSWERING HIS PHONE.
KANADE'S CONTACT SUGGESTS HE LEFT WILLINGLY.
WILL-INGLY?

BEFORE HE VANISHED, HE LEFT THIS BOOK OUT FOR US.
IT WAS OPEN TO THIS PHOTO OF A CLAY STATUETTE.
I THINK IT'S THE ANSWER TO THE FINGERNAIL MYSTERY.

PSYCHIC POWER
NANAKI™
CHRONICLE 9

YOU SAID...AO VANISHED?
YES.
JUST AS HE FIGURED OUT THE MYSTERY BEHIND THE CLIPPED FINGERNAILS.

IT'S AN EFFIGY USED FOR CURSING.
LIKE A VOODOO DOLL?

SOMETHING LIKE THAT. CLAY OR WOODEN EFFIGIES WERE USED FOR BLACK MAGIC IN ANCIENT INDIA, EGYPT, AND EUROPE AS WELL.
AND THIS UGLY STATUETTE HAS SOME-THING TO DO WITH IT?
HANG ON, OLD MAN!
HOW DO WE KNOW IT'S CONNECTED TO THIS CASE?
BECAUSE OF THE FINGER-NAILS.

YOU PUT SOMETHING FROM THE INTENDED VICTIM INSIDE THE EFFIGY.

THEN ANYTHING YOU DO TO IT HAPPENS TO THE PERSON.

Like poking its eyes out.

SOME-THING FROM THE INTENDED VICTIM?

LIKE A FINGER-NAIL...

...OR BLOOD...

...OR **HAIR!**

That's what Ao's book says.

THAT CREEP!

"IT MUST BE A SIGN THAT YOU SHOULD HAVE YOUR FORTUNE READ."

WHAT?

THIS CRYSTAL GAZER GUY GOT A HANK OF AO'S HAIR.

COME TO THINK OF IT, AO WAS ACTING WEIRDER THAN USUAL WHEN WE LEFT.

!

AO ALSO FOUND AN ACCIDENT REPORT FOR HIS SPOUSE.

SHE DROWNED ON VACATION, AT THE BEACH.

WAIT A MINUTE.

YOU DIDN'T TELL ANY-ONE...

...EVEN THOUGH YOU KNEW AO WAS ACTING STRANGELY?

WHAT'S YOUR DEAL?

YOU'VE BEEN GIVING ME DIRTY LOOKS SINCE THE MOMENT YOU LAID EYES ON ME.

IT'S BECAUSE YOU'RE NOT WORTHY TO BE AO'S PARTNER.

HUH?

IF *HE* HAD BEEN THERE, HE WOULDN'T HAVE JUST LEFT AO TO HIS FATE!

YOU'RE NOT *HALF* THE MAN NAOTO ISURUGI IS!

WHO ARE YOU TALKING ABOUT?!

There she goes again...

Uh-oh.

ISU-RUGI?
SO, THAT'S THE NAME OF AO'S EX-PARTNER WHO TURNED INTO A FREAK?
AO SAID HE DROPPED OUT AND VANISHED OF HIS OWN ACCORD.
THAT'S WHAT GUNJI-SAN SAID TOO!
BUT I REFUSE TO ACCEPT THAT!
I KNEW HIM. HE'D NEVER DOUBLE-CROSS AO!
HE'LL BE BACK, AND THEN YOU WON'T BE AO'S PARTNER ANYMORE.
OOH, SOMEONE'S GOT A CRUSH ON ISURUGI!
WHAT?! DO NOT!
OR MAYBE ON AO?
JUST...

JUST SHUT UP!

WE DON'T HAVE TIME FOR THIS!
EITHER HELP AO, OR GET OUT!

FINE. I'M OUTTA HERE.
HEY...!
WHAT? YOU'RE NOT GOING TO HELP AO?
I'M NOT GOOD ENOUGH, RIGHT?
VMMM
たすたす

WHAT A JERK!
VMMM
GUNJI-SAN, DO SOMETHING!
Aw, why did she have to start on about Isurugi?
JUST LET HIM GO.

I'M GOING TO CHECK IF MORIHIRO SAI IS AT THE FORTUNETELLING SHOP.

PRRRING

Fortune telling

CLICK

THIS IS THE FORTUNE MALL.

OH, ARE YOU FROM LOCK?

YES. IS SAI-SAN AVAILABLE?

I'M SORRY, BUT HE'S GONE HOME FOR THE NIGHT...

...LIKE I ALREADY TOLD YOUR INVESTIGATOR WHO CAME HERE.

!!

WAS HIS NAME AO KUDO?

UMM...

NO. IT WAS SHUNSUKE NANAKI-SAN.

I GAVE HIM A COPY OF THE STAFF LIST, AND HE LEFT.
OH. I'M SORRY TO BOTHER YOU.
THANK YOU FOR YOUR HELP.

SATSUKI.

IT'S TRUE THAT HE'S SOME-TIMES IRRE-SPONSIBLE...

...BUT APPARENTLY NOT THIS TIME.

DING-DONG

Takeko Kitami's episode: I admit that I love Takeko (lol). She was acting so freely that I almost thought, "how can I stop her?!" I wanted to bring out someone who's crazy about UFOs and supernatural beings, so I hope I was able to show her obsession (lol).

I gave her an older brother, and he's a freak in another way as well. Neither Nanaki nor Ao can defeat these two. I mean, Takeko already beat Nanaki by herself (lol)! She must be quite powerful to outwit him.

I also put a lizard with fake wings later in the episode, mainly because...I love lizards.

What?!

Really! I just love the little sounds they make. ← Over-excited

I found a picture of a UFO on the internet.

Seems like nobody's home.
OKAY.
POOF!
POOF!
UMPH!
HA! AND THEY SAY I NEED TRAINING.
You can't train genius.
HEY...
COOL STATUES!
!

...AO!!
HEY, AO, IT'S ME!
HE CAN'T BE...

すかー
WAKE UP!
ガッ

パチッ
NA-NAKI.
IS THAT ALL YOU HAVE TO SAY?
THE OLD MAN AND THE CHICKS ARE ON MY CASE.
Come back so I can tell them to shut up.
I CAN'T MOVE.
That's why I was sleeping.

IT MUST BE THE VOODOO DOLL! THAT GIRLY HAIR OF YOURS IS A LIABILITY.
Such a pain... Let me help you up.
I HAD NO CHOICE...
OBVI-OUSLY.

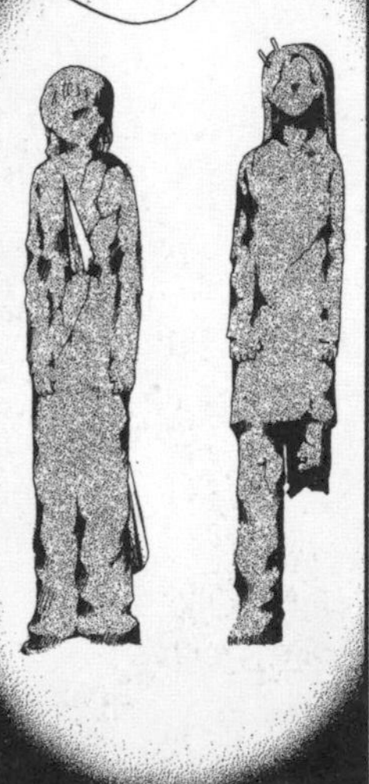
HE KEEPS MY EFFIGY WITH HIM.
THOSE OTHER TWO EFFIGIES BELONGED TO THE VICTIMS.

SO, SAI KILLED THEM.
DID THEY CATCH HIM TWO-TIMING?
NO. DIDN'T YOU READ THE ACCIDENT REPORT ON SAI'S WIFE?
You should read things I leave for you.

SHE DROWNED WHILE SWIMMING IN THE OCEAN ON VACATION.
See, I read some of it!
THE VICTIMS VACATIONED AT THE SAME PLACE.
AND THEY LET HER DIE.
!!

THE TWO OF THEM STOOD BY AND WATCHED HER DROWN.

LATER, WHEN THE BAD KARMA THAT CAUSED CAME BACK TO BITE THEM, THEY WANTED THEIR FORTUNES READ.

I SAID I NEEDED THEIR FINGERNAILS FOR MY READING.

SO YOU KILLED THEM FOR REVENGE? THAT'S HARSH, DUDE.
MAYBE THE VICTIMS DIDN'T REALIZE SHE WAS DROWNING.

A CON-VENIENT EXCUSE!
YEAH, YEAH, WE GET IT.
SO THEN YOU CURSED AO SO HE WOULDN'T ARREST YOU?
NO. I WANT TO HELP HIM.
...SAY WHAT?

YOU'VE LOST YOUR FORMER PARTNER AND CAN'T GET OVER IT.
YOU'RE STILL GRIEVING.

I'M NOT GRIEV-ING.
I'M JUST ANGRY AT HIM.

I KNOW HOW YOU FEEL.
IT'S A RARE GIFT TO FIND SOMEONE YOU SHARE A MUTUAL UNDERSTANDING WITH.
BOTH OF US HAVE FOUND AND LOST THAT PERSON.
STOP DENYING YOUR FEEL-INGS.
I SAW IT IN MY CRYSTAL BALL WHEN I MET YOU AT THE SHOP.
YOU HAVE THE MOST BEAUTIFUL SPIRIT I'VE EVER SEEN, BUT IT'S WOUNDED AND FULL OF SORROW.
I TOOK YOUR HAIR BECAUSE I WANTED TO FIND OUT WHY.

THAT'S WHEN I UNDER-STOOD. WE MUST LOOK FOR YOUR PARTNER.
IT'S OBVIOUS YOU BELONG WITH HIM.
MY PARTNER IS RIGHT HERE.
DON'T BE RIDICULOUS.
YOU TWO OBVIOUSLY CLASH IN EVERY WAY.
WHY WON'T YOU ADMIT IT?
!!

!!
ALL EVERYONE DOES IS COMPARE ME TO THIS GUY I'VE NEVER EVEN MET.
Knock it off!
I WAS NEVER GOING TO BE A CARBON COPY OF THAT GUY.
EXACTLY. YOU HAVE NO RIGHT TO CRITICIZE NANAKI'S WAY OF DOING THINGS.
AND NEITHER DO YOU.
Grrrr!
I DON'T GET IT. YOU HAD A BOND WITH YOUR FORMER PARTNER...
...LIKE I DID WITH MY WIFE.
WOULDN'T YOU WANT TO FIND SOMEONE MORE SIMILAR--
WAIT...

WHY COULDN'T YOU FORESEE YOUR WIFE'S DEATH?

PUTTING PEOPLE ON PEDESTALS WILL ONLY BRING PAIN.

IT'S UNFAIR TO NANAKI TO EVEN ***WONDER*** IF HE MEASURES UP!

CLUNK
YOU'RE MORE OF A FOOL THAN I THOUGHT.
THAT'S --!
IS THAT AO'S EFFIGY?!
YOU'VE CHOSEN POORLY.

WHAT A SHAME.

HEY, YOU OKAY?
?!
I CAN MOVE AGAIN ...?
OH, GOOD.
WHAT ?!
LEVEL ONE.
YOUR VOODOO DOLL HAS NO BATTERIES. I'VE GOT AO'S LOCK OF HAIR RIGHT HERE, LOSER.
The word you're looking for is G.E.N.I.U.S.! ♪

TELEPORTATION LEVEL ONE...
I WOULD'VE NEVER THOUGHT YOU WERE CAPABLE OF ACCURATELY REMOVING THE HAIR FROM INSIDE THE EFFIGY LIKE THAT.
It's a miracle.
YOU WANT ME TO PUT IT BACK?
Sheesh.
I MEAN--THANKS.
NO PROBLEM.
CRACK
"Crack"?

AO! ARE YOU ALL RIGHT?
HEY, GUYS!
What's up?
THEY BROKE DOWN THE DOOR!
Musta been a really cheap door.
SATSUKI HAS THE POWER OF MIGHTY ARM.
WHICH IS TO SAY, SHE HAS ENORMOUS STRENGTH ...
Ha ha ha!
THAT EXPLAINS WHY SHE REMINDS ME OF A GORILLA!
YOU JUST SHUT UP!
NANAKI-KUN, KUDO-KUN...

YOU WIN.

IT WAS NEVER ABOUT WINNING OR LOSING.
NO...
I'VE UNDER-ESTIMATED YOU.
I BELIEVED YOU TWO WOULD NEVER BE COMPATIBLE.
BUT IT SEEMS YOU BOTH HAVE HIDDEN DEPTHS.

WE'RE ONLY CHARGING MORIHIRO SAI WITH THE FALSE IMPRISON-MENT OF AO.
WHAT?!

WHAT ABOUT THOSE TWO DEAD CHICKS?
HE'S PLEADING INNO-CENT.
AND MURDER OR ATTEMPTED MURDER BY CURSING IS VERY DIFFICULT TO PROVE.
SO HE'S GETTING AWAY WITH IT?

THAT JERK ADMITTED THE CRIME, AND NOW HE'S GOING BACK ON THAT.
Jeez!
IT'S IN HEAD-QUARTERS' HANDS NOW.
LEAVING US FREE TO TALK ABOUT YOUR PARTNERSHIP ISSUES.
WHAT?

SATSUKI, YOU REFUSED TO ACCEPT THEM AS A TEAM, RIGHT?
!
YES, I DID.
SO, HAS YOUR OPINION CHANGED?
HE'S OBVIOUSLY INEXPERI-ENCED.
HEY! SHE'S STARTING AGAIN!
—
...BUT HE IMMEDIATELY WENT TO AO'S RESCUE.
I'M NOT SAYING MORIHIRO SAI IS RIGHT, BUT...

LET'S JUST SAY...
...I'LL GIVE HIM NO MORE TROUBLE ABOUT BEING AO'S PARTNER.
THANKS FOR THE VOTE OF CONFIDENCE.
Sheesh.
DON'T PUSH IT!
ISN'T THAT GREAT, AO?! ♫
......

PSYCHIC POWER
NANAKI™
CHRONICLE 10

AAAH!
HOT SPRINGS ARE AWE-SOME!

KICK

WHOA!

ぷはっ

WHAT THE HELL?!

HOW LONG ARE YOU GOING TO STAY IN THERE?
ザワ…ッ
THIS ISN'T A VACATION, YOU KNOW.
AO...

WHAT DID YOU KICK ME FOR?!
HEY, MISS! THE WOMEN'S BATH IS OVER THERE!
Yikes!
Don't look!
Noo!

BUT YOU'RE MORE THAN WELCOME TO SLIP OUT OF THAT ROBE AND COME ON IN, MISS.

JUST GET OUT OF THE BATH.
I WANT TO GET TO WORK.

....
HEY, STOP FREAKING OUT. HE'S A GUY!
They're not listening...
NOW I UNDERSTAND WHY YOU AVOID THE OUTDOOR BATH...
She's way too hot for me.
Wish I was young.
Lucky guy.

WHICH ONE?
HER.
MIKA ISHIKAWA.

DIDN'T YOU READ THE FILE? THERE WAS A PICTURE IN IT.
YEAH, YEAH. SHE MIGHT BE A PSYCHIC, RIGHT?
I REMEMBER WHAT THE OLD MAN SAID IN THE BRIEFING.

YOU KNOW OF THE RECENT INCIDENTS, I PRESUME?

A FIRE AT AN ITALIAN RESTAURANT IN SHIBUYA, AND A BUS ACCIDENT.

CORRECT. THE FIRE STARTED IN THE RESTAURANT'S KITCHEN.

AND THE BUS ACCIDENT WAS DUE TO THE DRIVER HAVING AN APNEA ATTACK.

SO WHY DO WE CARE?

BLIP

THE POLICE FOUND NO FOUL PLAY IN EITHER CASE, BUT LOOK AT THIS.

LOOKS LIKE A FORUM.

[6421] Warning

Anonymous 02/21 (Sat) 10:03

Tomorrow from 3:00 to 4:00 p.m., avoid the Italian restaurant in Spain-zaka, Shibuya.

THAT'S EXACTLY WHAT IT IS.

[6733] Warning

Anonymous 03/19 (Fri) 14:28

Don't take the Nakameguro Station to Ohimachi bus on the 23rd, 11 a.m. to 1 p.m.

SECOND SIGHT?
WHAT?

EVERY ONE WAS WRITTEN BY THE SAME HIGH SCHOOL GIRL:

...MIKA ISHIKAWA.

YOU WILL INVESTIGATE IF THE PERSON POSTING THESE WARNINGS IS A PSYCHIC.

Warning

Anonymous 03/21 (Sun) 08:15

Watch out for the store sign near Ohmiya Train Station in Saitama Prefecture on the evening of the 25th.

...SO ANYWAY...

!

?

WHAT'S UP WITH HER?

RUSTLE

SHE LOOKS LIKE SHE'S TRYING TO HIDE FROM SOMEONE.

SHE SEEMS TO BE WATCHING...

...THAT GUY.
WHO'S THAT?
DON'T KNOW.
......
LET'S FIND OUT!
!!
YO, DUDE, YOU HERE BY YOUR-SELF?
?!
NANAKI, YOU IDIOT!

The curse episode: The remaining First Division members, Satsuki and Kanade, have finally made their appearance. They were originally planned to be twin sisters. However, I decided to nix the idea in favor of the twin brother story in volume one instead.

It was easy to come up with Satsuki's character sketch, but I kept changing Kanade's until the last minute. I even had trouble deciding her name, too!

Morihiro Sai is basically a serious character, but I'd probably have the same reaction as Nanaki and Ao if he grabbed my hair.

Speaking of which, I couldn't decide what to do with Ao's hair when he was sleeping in Sai's house... I thought it would bother him if he slept with a ponytail (lol)! I know it means nothing, but it bugged me so much. I ended up having Sai undo his ponytail before laying him down... Oh gosh, I can imagine Ao giving him such a disgusted look (nervous laugh)!

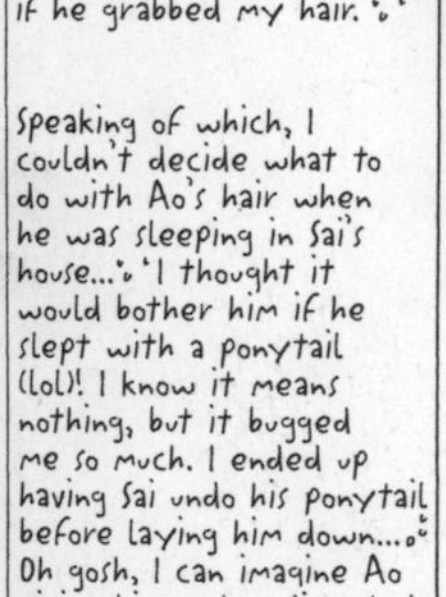

WHERE DID YOU POP UP FROM, KID?

YOU GONNA TRY AND SELL ME SOMETHING?

NAH. I'M JUST BORED.

YOU DIDN'T SEEM BUSY, SO I DECIDED TO TALK TO YOU.

Their Everyday Conversation

Ah ha ha ha ha ha!
Hey, on the TV they were telling everyone to get high and go surfing!
Um, that's "high surf advisory"...

BOREDOM IS NO EXCUSE FOR RUDENESS.
I'M TRYING TO RELAX.
Got it?
WHATEVER.
Well, they're getting on famously.
EXCUSE ME.

DO YOU KNOW DOC?
!
IT'S MIKA ISHIKAWA!

DOC?
Back when I was in high school, kids didn't all carry cell phones.
Huh? No way! How old are you?
THAT'S WHAT PEOPLE CALL HIM.
I DON'T KNOW WHAT HIS REAL NAME IS, THOUGH.

WHAT NATIONALITY IS HE?

I HEARD HE'S JAPANESE...
WAIT! YOU DON'T KNOW HIM?

A NICK-NAME. HMM.
NOT AT ALL.
OH, I'M SORRY. I ASSUMED YOU DID...
YOO-HOO!

UH ... WELL ...
I THINK THEY'RE ASKING YOU OUT.
NO, WE MEAN BOTH OF YOU!

GET OUT OF MY FACE.

THAT'S RIGHT. YOU REALLY WANT A FLAT-CHESTED GIRL LIKE THIS?

Size matters.

WHERE DID YOU COME FROM?!

AND THE OTHER ONE'S UNDERAGE. YOU LIKE JAIL?

Huh?

SEE HERE, NANAKI.

WHAT, DOC?

ザワ

YOU'RE SO INSENSITIVE.

WHAT?!

ザワ

DON'T LET HIM BOTHER YOU, MISS.

ポンッ

YOU'RE STILL ATTRACTIVE, EVEN WITH YOUR FLAT CHEST.

Like that would be reassuring.

Err...

HEY, DOC? DUCK.
ONE REQUEST.
?!
YES?
And besides, you didn't ask until after you swung.
LET ME PUNCH YOU.
NO THANKS. I'M NOT FOND OF PAIN.

Oh.

IT'S YOU, MIKA-CHAN.

ARE YOU ALL RIGHT? YOU'RE NOT HURT?

I'M FINE. HEY, WHERE DID THOSE OTHER GUYS GO?

THOSE IDIOTS? THEY'RE GONE.

THEY LEFT.

Finally.

ANYWAY, WHAT A PLEASANT SURPRISE.

YOU'RE VACATIONING HERE TOO?

*Note: A baku is a Japanese spirit animal who eats bad dreams.

PLEASE, YOU'RE IN DANGER. MY DREAMS ALWAYS COME TRUE.
IN THAT CASE ...
...BRING IT ON.

PREMONITION AND PREDICTION ARE HARDLY DEFINITE SCIENCES.
BESIDES...
I DON'T BELIEVE IN FATE.

TAKE CARE, MIKA-CHAN.

SEE YA, NANAKI-KUN, AO-KUN.

DOC!

HE'S JUST LIKE YOU.

HUH?

FULL OF HIM-SELF.

YOU--!

......

HE WON'T... BELIEVE ME...

......

I'm not surprised.

MAN, IS NEWS ALL THEY SHOW ON TV HERE?

I-I'M SORRY.

FLIP

The sweet taste that's all the rage! Try some today!

WHAT ARE YOU APOLOGIZING FOR?

I-I DON'T KNOW. I'M SORRY.

UM...YOU SAID YOU WANTED TO SPEAK TO ME?

First...

WHAT'S YOUR RELATIONSHIP WITH "DOC"?

HUH?!

H-HE'S A REGULAR AT THE CAFÉ WHERE I WORK!

OH! BUT HE CAME TO MY DEFENSE ONCE WHEN I ACCIDENTALLY SPILLED COFFEE ON A CUSTOMER.

あわわ

わわ

That's all, honest!

CALM DOWN.

フッ

heh

SO BASICALLY...

フフッ

heh heh!

YOU HAVE A CRUSH ON HIM AND FOLLOWED HIM HERE, RIGHT?
WHAT?!
IT'S WRITTEN ALL OVER YOUR FACE.
......
You should learn from Ao, he's Mr. Poker Face.
......
NOW, AN UPDATE ON THE ACCIDENT REPORTED EARLIER.
OUR CORRES-PONDENT, SAGAWA, IS NEAR THE SCENE AT OHMIYA TRAIN STATION.
!!

THE SIGN THAT FELL DOWN AROUND 4:10 P.M. WAS PLACED ON DISPLAY THREE DAYS AGO TO PROMOTE A SALE.

AN OFFICIAL LATER STATED THAT IT MAY HAVE BEEN SECURED IMPROPERLY.

SO FAR, THE INJURY COUNT IS...

SONY

ARE THEY SERIOUS? THEY AREN'T JUST MAKING THIS UP?

...I GUESS NOT.

SO MIKA'S POST WAS FOR REAL, AGAIN.

WHAT THE...?!

CHILL OUT.

WE'RE FROM LOCK.

WE INVESTIGATE SUPERNATURAL EVENTS.

SUPER-NATURAL?!

WE KNOW YOU CAN PREDICT THE FUTURE.
TEAR
UGH!

COME ON, MIKA.
WHY ARE YOU CRYING?
AO, DO SOMETHING.
BUT YOU'RE DOING SUCH A BRILLIANT JOB WITH YOUR YAPPING.

Talking telepathically.

......
SHUT UP! I DON'T KNOW HOW TO DEAL WITH NICE GIRLS.
BLUNTLY.
....
MY DREAMS ...
...KEEP COMING TRUE. AGAIN AND AGAIN.

I USED TO TELL MY PARENTS ABOUT THEM, BUT WHEN SO MANY OF MY DREAMS BECAME REALITY IN EVERY DETAIL...
...I COULD TELL THEY THOUGHT I WAS CREEPY, EVEN THOUGH THEY DIDN'T SAY ANYTHING.

WHEN I STOPPED MENTION-ING IT...
...THEY WERE SO MUCH HAPPIER.
I'VE NEVER TOLD ANY-ONE SINCE.

THEN WHY DID YOU MAKE THOSE POSTS ON THAT FORUM?

I THOUGHT MAYBE I COULD PREVENT DISASTERS...
...IF PEOPLE WERE WARNED IN AD-VANCE.
BUT NO ONE WOULD BELIEVE ME. I DIDN'T SAVE A SINGLE LIFE. I'M SO...

...USELESS.

THERE MUST BE A BRIGHT SIDE!
LIKE GETTING WINNING LOTTERY NUMBERS.
OR TEST QUESTIONS.
......
...I WISH THAT WERE TRUE.
BUT I ONLY EVER DREAM ABOUT TRAGEDIES.
WHAT?
THAT REMINDS ME--YOU HAD A DREAM ABOUT DOC, RIGHT?
....
YES.

IN THAT DREAM I SAW...

...THIS HOT SPRING RESORT...

...AND A CAVE.

DOC WAS IN THE CAVE, AND A ROCK FELL ON HIS HEAD.
HE WAS COVERED IN BLOOD.

MY PREDICTIONS...
...HAVE BEEN 100 PERCENT ACCURATE ONLY WHEN THEY INVOLVE SOMEONE'S DEATH.

PSYCHIC POWER
NANAKI™
CHRONICLE 11

MY DREAMS ONLY COME TRUE WHEN SOMEONE'S LIFE IS IN DANGER.
I'M SO FRIGHTENED THAT DOC WILL BE KILLED IN THAT CAVE!

THAT JERK!
WHY COULDN'T HE JUST SLEEP IN LIKE A NORMAL PERSON?
BUT AT LEAST THE FRONT DESK GUY REMEM-BERED HE'D MENTIONED A CAVE.

THE HOURS YOU KEEP ARE YOUR OWN FAULT.
SLEEP RULES.

BUT MIKA, SHOULDN'T YOU HAVE STAYED AT THE INN?
Getting to the cave will be a pain.
I'M FINE, THANKS!
I CAN'T STAY THERE BY MYSELF, WORRYING.
BESIDES, I GOT YOU INTO THIS.
WE WERE HARDLY DRAGGED INTO IT.
RELAX. EVERYTHING WILL BE COOL.
YOU THINK SO?

IS THIS IT?
WHOA!
YES!
DEF-INITELY!
THIS IS THE CAVE I SAW IN MY DREAM.
THEN LET'S GO SEE WHAT'S UP, DOC!
MAN, I KILL ME--

RUMBLE
YOWCH!

OH NO! THE EN-TRANCE!

UGH. SUCH A STUPID PLACE FOR A ROCK TO STICK OUT...
......

HEY, NANAKI. YOU DIDN'T DO THAT ON PURPOSE, DID YOU?
HUH ?!
THE ENTRANCE IS COMPLETELY BLOCKED NOW.

AND THAT ROCK NEARLY BROKE MY HEAD OPEN!
I HOPE IT KNOCKED SOME SENSE INTO YOU.
Midgets like you wouldn't notice!
You--!

THESE ROCKS SEEM PRE-CARIOUS.
AND DON'T TALK SO LOUDLY.
WHAT?
CHILL. I'LL TAKE CARE OF IT.
JUST RELAX AND WATCH THE GENIUS WORK.
C'MON.
NANAKI IS REALLY CONFIDENT, ISN'T HE?
...YEAH.
HE THINKS HE CAN HOLD THE ROCKS UP WITH HIS PSI?

OH!

WELL, THAT EXPLAINS WHERE THE LIGHT WAS COMING FROM.

HM?
NANAKI-KUN! WHAT A SURPRISE.
IT MUST BE FATE.
FATE MY ASS. WE WERE LOOKING FOR YOU.
WHY ARE YOU HERE?
DON'T TELL ME YOU'RE JUST A CAVE NUT.
OH, NO.
I'M HERE TO MEET SOME-ONE.

WE MUST HAVE MISSED EACH OTHER.
I HOPE NOTHING HAPPENED...
WHAT DO YOU MEAN?
HM?
WELL, I'M DONE HERE, SO LET'S GO.
YOU'RE IGNORING ME!
I'll buy you something at the gift shop on the way back.
BUT DOC, THE ENTRANCE IS BLOCKED BY A CAVE-IN!
WHAT?

OH NO! SO, DO THE TWO OF YOU HAVE A PLAN FOR GETTING OUT?
HUH?
DON'T TELL ME YOU TWO CAME OUT HERE WITH MIKA...
...STUPIDLY ASSUMING THERE WOULDN'T BE ANY RISK.

HEY!

NANAKI, DON'T!

POOF!
NANAKI!
You didn't go anywhere.
WHAT THE HELL?! I DIDN'T MEAN TO DO THAT.
HOW ODD. YOU'VE NEVER HAD A PROBLEM LIKE THAT BEFORE.
MAYBE THIS AREA HAS A STRONG MAGNETIC FIELD.
WHOA!
WHAT?
THE EARTH'S MAGNETIC FIELD.
ITS FREQUENCY FLUCTUATES DEPENDING ON WHAT IT'S PASSING THROUGH, BUT IT'S STRONGER IN CAVES AND VOLCANIC REGIONS.
STRONG ELECTRO-MAGNETIC FIELDS AFFECT THE HUMAN BODY AND INHIBIT PSYCHIC POWER.

E-EXCUSE ME.
CARE TO EXPLAIN WHAT JUST HAPPENED?

CRAP.
LIKE MIKA, WE ALSO HAVE SPECIAL ABILITIES.
Sheesh.

YOU DO?!
YEAH, BUT MAGNETIC FIELDS WEREN'T PART OF MY PLAN.
YOU? MADE A PLAN?
WAIT. WHO DO YOU GUYS WORK FOR?
OH, FORGET IT.
WAIT A MINUTE, NANAKI.
WHAT ARE YOU DOING?
CAN'T YOU GUESS?

I'M GOING TO CLIMB OUT OF HERE.
!!
I'LL TELEPORT PART OF THE WAY, THOUGH.
Man, I hope this works.
HELP WILL GET HERE FASTER IF I BRING IT BACK WITH ME.
BESIDES, WE NEED TO GET OUT OF THIS CAVE BEFORE YOUR DREAM COMES TRUE.
You can sit here and wait on fate.
!!
B-BUT...
PLEASE, STOP!
IT'S TOO DANGEROUS! WE SHOULD WAIT FOR HELP!
SEE, PSYCHIC POWER IS JUST AN ADDED BONUS FOR ME.

LONG AGO I LEARNED TO RELY ON...
...WHAT I CAN GRAB ONTO WITH MY OWN HANDS.
OKAY, LET'S DO IT!

Pof!
AW, CRAP!
!!
POOF!
Goal
NANAKI-SAN!
I NEED TO GET CLOSER...
...TO THE CLIFF!
Trying again.
POOF!

NANAKI THINKS HE CAN FIX EVERYTHING HIMSELF.
BUT I'M THE OPPOSITE. I COULD NEVER PREVENT THE PREMONITIONS FROM COMING TRUE BY MYSELF.
ALL RIGHT! UP I GO!
I SEE.
I KNOW, I KNOW ...

WHAT'S THIS?

POP

The precognitive dream episode: I never had a precognitive dream, though I've heard of people winning lotteries with numbers they saw in their dreams... I'm so jealous of them.

Since the episode takes place at a hot spring, I dressed up Nanaki and Ao in yukata. My friends who saw the scene where Ao kicks Nanaki told me I should expose more of Ao's leg. They said Ao would be cool as a samurai with a sword, or as a yakuza wife. They just went bonkers with suggestions.

Some readers requested fanservice pictures of Ao, but I'm sorry. I'm afraid he'd look so sexy that I just can't do it. Please don't get upset with me. I ran out of space for Doc, so I'll talk about him in the next free talk (lol)!

I was wearing a white coat when I met Gunji, but I'm not a doctor.

DOC!

MIKA!
HEY!
WHAT JUST HAP-PENED?!

I CAN'T BELIEVE I LET A NOTE DISTRACT ME FROM A FALLING ROCK.
I'M SORRY, MIKA.
......?!

POOF

?!

HANG ON! THIS IS...

...OUR ROOM BACK AT THE INN?!

UGH...

MIKA!

PLEASE TAKE CARE OF HER.

YOU --

すたすた

CLICK

HEY, YOU'RE GONNA JUST WALK OUT AND ABANDON MIKA?!

YES. IT'S BEST SHE DOESN'T GET INVOLVED WITH ME ANYMORE.

WHAT?!

YOU AREN'T GOING ANYWHERE, CREEP!

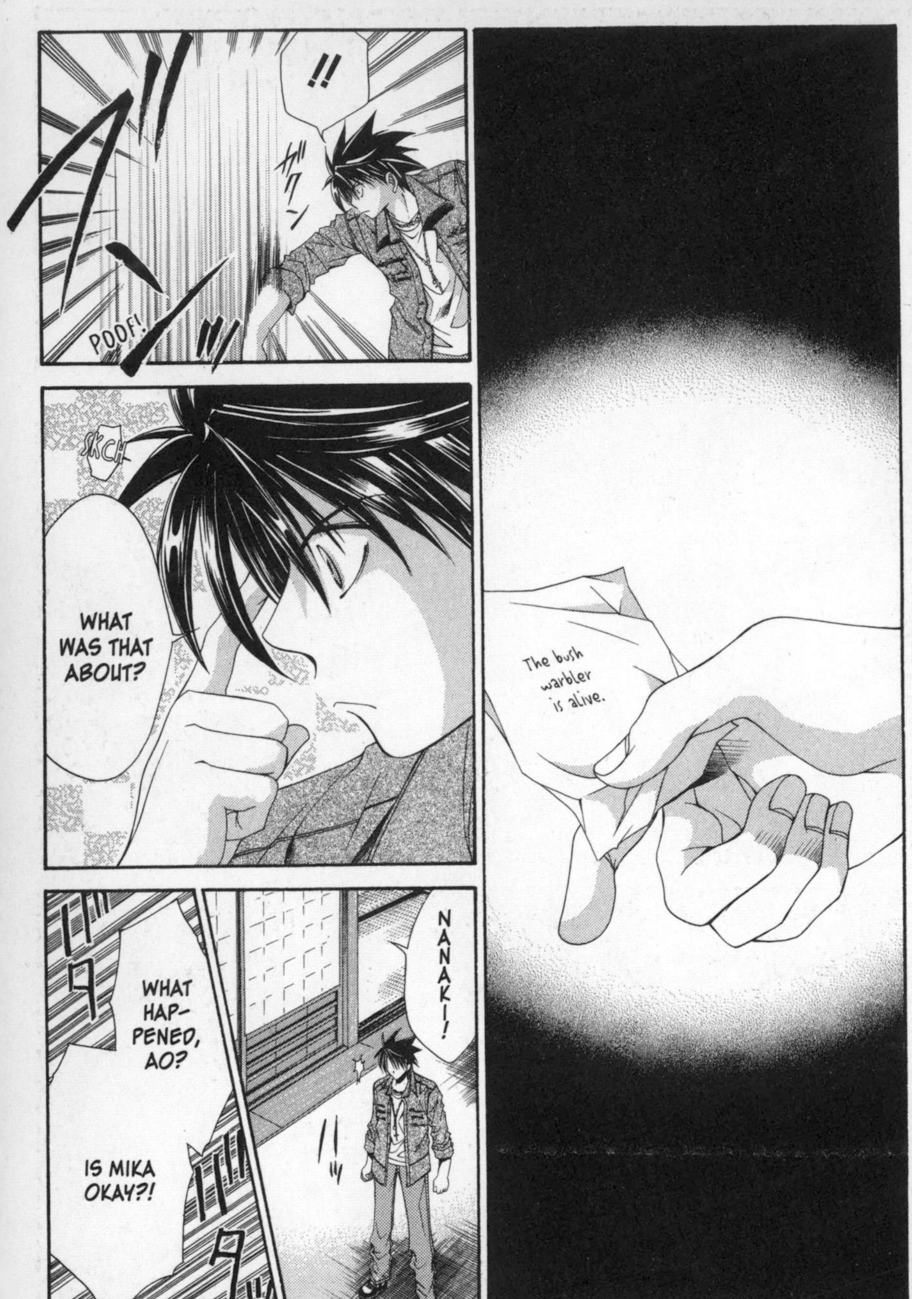
The bush warbler is alive.
!!
POOF!
SKCH
WHAT WAS THAT ABOUT?
NANAKI!
WHAT HAPPENED, AO?
IS MIKA OKAY?!

MIKA!
I'M SORRY FOR ALL THE TROUBLE.
UM, NANAKI-SAN, WHERE'S DOC?
HE TOOK OFF.
IS HE ALL RIGHT?
WHAT?
THANK GOD.
WHAT?!
HE'S RIGHT AS RAIN!
YOU SAVED HIS LIFE, AND HE BUGGERS OFF WITHOUT EVEN A THANKS!
もっと切れろ!!
You should be furious!!
IT'S OKAY!!

BECAUSE...
...I WAS ABLE TO DEFEAT ONE OF MY PREMONITIONS.
AND I OWE EVERYTHING TO YOU...
...NANAKI-SAN.

I HAVE AN UPDATE ON MIKA ISHIKAWA'S CASE.

OUR TEST DETERMINED THAT SHE'S NOT PSYCHIC.
WHAT?!

WE SUSPECT ANY ABILITIES WERE CURTAILED BY HER RECENT HEAD TRAUMA.
む
SO SHE'S BACK TO NORMAL, HUH?
What are you calling normal, freak?

THEREFORE HER MEMORY HAS BEEN ERASED.
?!
WHAT?!

AS FOR THE MAN CALLED DOC...

WE DON'T HAVE ANY INFORMATION ON HIM.

OTHER THAN THAT HIS NICKNAME IS SHORT FOR "DOCTOR," OF COURSE.

?

HOW DO YOU KNOW?

BECAUSE I GAVE IT TO HIM.
DO WHAT?
HE USED TO SHOW UP AT THE SAME CRIME SCENES HARUKA AND I WOULD BE ASSIGNED TO.
HE GOT THAT NICKNAME FROM THE WHITE COAT HE WAS WEARING WHEN WE FIRST MET.
He never told us his real name, either.
DAMN IT.
I CLIMBED UP THAT MASSIVE CLIFF BECAUSE OF HIM...
NEXT TIME I SEE HIM, I'M GONNA POP HIM!
ME FIRST.
YOU TWO...

PSYCHIC POWER NANAKI™

CHRONICLE 12

DOMINION!

IF I WERE A REAL ENEMY, IT WOULD'VE BEEN...

ARGH!

...SO IT SEEMS.

I TOLD YOU IT WAS IMPOSSIBLE.
YOU CAN'T BEAT A HIGH-LEVEL TELEKENESIS USER. IT'S THE KING OF PSYCHIC ABILITIES.

BUT DOMINION IS A FORM OF PSYCHOKINESIS. CAN'T I--
CAN'T YOU USE BARRIER TO BLOCK TELEKINESIS, YOU WANT TO SAY?

YEAH.

BARRIER WILL CERTAINLY PREPARE YOU TO HANDLE A PK ATTACK...

...BUT IT WON'T GIVE YOU ANY SUSTAINED DEFENSIVE POWER.

YOU'VE TOLD ME THAT BEFORE.

AO, YOU'RE A HEALER FIRST AND FOREMOST.

YOUR SECONDARY ABILITIES IN DOMINION, GHOST SIGHT AND SPIRITUAL BLOW ARE ALREADY PRETTY STRONG.

I got Spiritual Blow too, 'cause I'm a genius. ♪

YOU SHOULD WORK ON ENHANCING YOUR DOMINION SKILLS INSTEAD OF CHASING A NEW POWER.

TRY TO TRANSFORM THAT FAN INTO SOMETHING OTHER THAN A POLE.

......

He got me there.

A HAUNTED BUILDING.

THIS INN WAS CLOSED DOWN LAST YEAR AFTER A FOOD POISONING OUTBREAK.

I HEARD RUMORS THAT A GHOST HAS BEEN SIGHTED HERE.

That's fairly common with abandoned buildings.

ANYWAY, WHY ARE YOU COMING WITH ME?
YOUR TEAMMATE ISN'T OUT OF SCHOOL FOR ANOTHER FEW HOURS.
LOCK POLICY IS FOR TWO AGENTS TO ATTEND ANY INVESTIGATION.
I'M HERE FOR PERSONAL CURIOSITY, NOT FOR LOCK.

I'M YOUR GUARDIAN.

I'M 20.

GOD, YOU'RE WORSE THAN NANAKI.

YOU HAVEN'T TOLD NANAKI ABOUT YOUR CONDITION?

IT MIGHT STOP HIM TREATING YOU LIKE A LITTLE KID.

HIM, CHANGE HIS ATTITUDE?

I doubt that.

HEH, YOU MAY BE RIGHT.

KRAK
!
WHAT IS IT?
TAP
I HEARD SOME-THING.
!!
HELP
PLIP

In my preliminary rough sketch of Doc, he had a slightly long ponytail but I changed it. His name was meant to be a way of addressing him like a master rather than an abbreviation of "doctor." When I think about it now, I have a feeling there was a TV drama with this name as a title...

The haunted building episode: This was created as a counterpart to Takeko's episode, which was mainly about Nanaki. Gunji and Ao have known each other for a long time. Since they live in the LOCK First Division residential area, they often have meals together (lol). As far as Shingo Marunouchi is concerned, well...I like him (lol). He's a real coward, but he has a positive attitude. I understand this feeling, since I used to be a chicken when I was younger, too.

Hey, the big boss is staring at you.

So? I don't care.

↑ They're on their way to the general meeting at LOCK headquarters... Ao did his best to dress up for the occasion. He'll continue to ignore the warnings from HQ about his dress for the next meeting, too (nervous laugh)...

WHAT THE...

HELP

Spray paint
スプレーペイント
OH, MAN.
THIS PICTURE'S GONNA BE SO GOOD.
....

I'M SHINGO MARUNO-UCHI.

Heh!

Eh

I'M A JOURNALIST AT ***QUEERNESS***, A MYSTERY MAGAZINE!

あわ
あわわわ
PLEASE DON'T TELL ANYONE! I'LL LOSE MY JOB IF I DON'T COME BACK WITH AN INTERESTING STORY!
......
YOU DON'T BELIEVE ME?
HERE. MY BUSINESS CARD, AND MY DRIVER'S LICENCE.
...AO.
YOUR TURN. WHO THE HECK ARE YOU?
HAVE YOU HEARD OF A SHINGO MARUNOUCHI WORKING FOR QUEERNESS MAGAZINE?
? ?

I'M AO KUDO, AND THIS IS HIDEAKI GUNJI.
WE'RE FROM THE PARANORMAL TASK FORCE.
...THE PARANORMAL ENTHUSIASTS GROUP, LOCK?!
PARA-NORMAL?
N-NO WAY! YOU'RE...
どずーーん
...ENTHUSIASTS GROUP?
SO...
WE'RE LIKE SOME KIND OF FAN CLUB?
ALL RIGHT! I'VE ALWAYS WANTED TO MEET YOU GUYS!
HEY, IS IT OKAY IF I FOLLOW YOU AROUND?!
...WHAT?
C'MON!
I LOVE MYSTERIES!
CREAK
BUT I--

YIKES!

I-I'M A T-TOTAL CHICKEN.

WE GOT US A CHICKEN.

So why is he a journalist for a mystery magazine?

A CHICKEN, HUH?

why not?

BUT...I REALLY *LIKE* BEING FRIGHT-ENED.

OTHERWISE I WOULDN'T BE IN THIS LINE OF WORK!

I GET IT ALREADY.

Shut up...

HUH?

IF IT'S WHAT YOU REALLY WANT...
...YOU CAN COME WITH US.
I CAN? THANKS SO MUCH, KUDO-KUN!
Woohoo!
ぶん
ぶん
I'M GOING TO WAIT IN THE CAR.
AO.
OKAY.

FORGET ABOUT IT. LET'S GO.
Gunji-saaan!
WHAT?
DID I UPSET HIM?!

PER-HAPS...
...I MEDDLED TOO MUCH IN HIS BUSI-NESS.
OH! WAIT A MINUTE, KUDO-KUN!

HMM.
WE'RE NOT FINDING ANYTHING.

HEY, KUDO-KUN, LOCK ONLY INVESTIGATES WHEN THERE'S CLEAR EVIDENCE, RIGHT?
WRONG.

I'M HERE ON MY OWN TIME.
EH?
BUT YOU BELIEVE IN THE SUPERNATURAL, DON'T YOU?! I BET YOU'VE WITNESSED LOTS OF AMAZING STUFF!
I'VE NEVER SEEN ANY-THING.
blah
blah
DO YOU EVER SHUT UP?
Someone else talks as much as Nanaki?
blah
YEAH, I'VE NEVER EVEN MET A LOCK AGENT BEFORE YOU!
I HEARD ABOUT YOU, BUT I WASN'T SURE IF YOU TRULY EXISTED.
I SEE.
BUT WAIT. HOW OLD ARE YOU?
20.
REALLY? YOU DON'T LOOK YOUR AGE.
I'M JEALOUS! I'LL BE 25 THIS YEAR, BUT IT FEELS LIKE THE YEARS ARE SPEEDING UP.
DO YOU HATE IT?
HATE WHAT?
THE WAY TIME PASSES.

NOT REALLY! I COULDN'T WAIT TO GET OLDER!
I THOUGHT I COULD GROW OUT OF BEING A CHICKEN.
I never did, though.
MY LATEST GOAL IS TO DO SOMETHING ABOUT IT BEFORE I TURN 30!
I'D HATE TO MISS MY BIG SHOT AT SEEING A GHOST BECAUSE I WAS TOO SCARED.
ME TOO.
WHAT?
I COULDN'T WAIT TO GROW UP EITHER.
REALLY? JUST LIKE ME! WE'RE GONNA BE BEST FRIENDS!

RIGHT? ♬
I'LL FULFILL YOUR WISH.

?
KUDO-KUN?
ぐいっ

OBSERVE CLOSELY.

WHAT'RE YOU DOING?! OHMIGOD, IT LOOKS LIKE YOU CUT AN ARTERY!
WHA--!

IT'S THE ONLY THING I'M GOOD AT.

...THANKS.

GOOD ENOUGH!

WEIRDO. A GHOST OBSESSED WITH THE SUPER-NATURAL...

THAT'S THE THING!

YOU GUYS SPOKE NORMALLY TO ME! THAT WAS COOL.

WELL, I DID. BUT GUNJI-SAN COULDN'T SEE YOU.

He couldn't hear you either.

WHAT? ARE YOU SERIOUS?!

I DIED BEFORE DOING WHAT I WANTED WITH LIFE. I DIDN'T KNOW WHAT TO DO.

I COULDN'T FEEL READY TO MOVE ON UNTIL I'D SEEN A SUPERNATURAL PHENOMENON.

Really!

THANKS A LOT, KUDO-KUN!

YOU DON'T NEED TO THANK ME.

I wasn't much help.

HEY, KUDO-KUN, DON'T TALK LIKE THAT!

YOU CAME ALL THE WAY HERE BECAUSE YOU WANTED TO HELP OUT A GHOST, RIGHT?

......

WELL, WITH A POWER LIKE THAT, YOU PROBABLY USUALLY GET STUCK USING IT IN A SUPPORT ROLE!

Ah ha ha ha ha ha ha!

WHY, YOU...

BUT YOU KNOW...

YOU SHOULDN'T BE MISLED BY YOUR NAME, ***ETERNAL IMMATURITY.***

!

HOW DID YOU--

*One meaning of the kanji used in his name.

I GOT A HINT ABOUT YOUR CURSE...
Ha ha!
...WHEN WE WERE TALKING ABOUT OUR AGES!
DON'T LOSE HOPE ON LIFTING THE CURSE, THOUGH!
I'M OUT OF TIME HERE, BUT I HOPE YOU FIND THAT PERSON WHO CAN HELP YOU.

SOMEONE WHO CAN BE YOUR GUIDING LIGHT.

YOU SOUND LIKE YOU'RE TALKING TO YOURSELF.
GUNJI-SAN!
I RAN A BACKGROUND CHECK IN MY CAR.
SHINGO MARUNOUCHI WAS INDEED A JOURNAL-IST FOR *QUEERNESS* MAGAZINE.

FIVE DAYS AGO, HE WAS ON HIS WAY HERE TO RESEARCH THIS BUILDING--WHEN HE CRASHED HIS MOTORCYCLE AND DIED.

THEY'RE BACK! AO-KUN!

GUNJI-SAN!

UMMM

WHAT TOOK YOU SO LONG?

YOU DON'T KNOW WHAT WE'VE BEEN THROUGH!

......?

つかつか

つかつかつか

WE TRIED TO CALL YOU.

I TOLD HIM YOU TWO WERE TOGETHER, BUT HE WOULDN'T LISTEN...

AH!

HEY.
NANAKI!
WHA ...
IS THAT ALL YOU HAVE TO SAY FOR YOURSELF?
EVERYBODY'S OKAY, ♫ NANAKI-KUN.
See?
I TOLD YOU HE WASN'T IN DANGER.
PLEASE. WHAT'S GOING ON?

YOU CALLED OUT TO ME THROUGH TELEPATHY.
WHAT HAPPENED?
"YOU SHOULDN'T BE MISLED BY YOUR NAME, ETERNAL IMMATURITY."
"I'M OUT OF TIME HERE, BUT I HOPE YOU FIND THAT PERSON WHO CAN HELP YOU."
DID SOMEONE THREATEN YOU?
...BEING MY GUIDING LIGHT IS ANOTHER MATTER.
HUH?

I DOUBT I'LL EVER BREAK FREE OF THE INFLUENCE OF MY NAME...

...BUT THE ONLY PERSON WHO CAME TO MIND AT THAT MOMENT WAS...

...SHUNSUKE NANAKI.

TO BE CONTINUED...

I Can Do It Myself.

※Title

Read from right to left panels.

Wassup.

Huh? Where did these homeboys crawl out from?
They're investigators from LOCK's Kansai Branch.

Word! I'm Ryota Kamo, and stone-face over here is Tsuzuru Uesugi-kun.
Nice to meet ya.
Long time no see, Ao-kun.
What? Least I don't wear a diaper on my head.
So you're Nanaki, the newbie?

Don't get fresh with me, retard. I'm gonna pop you.
Pop what, one of your zits?
East-West Standoff
What should we do, Ao-kun?
Just ignore them.
The same age.

Ao! Don't you care about your partner?
Go stop 'em now, or your unit is toast!
You stop them.
...You just don't wanna be bothered.

Then let's have a lunch bento box showdown!
Shut up, Kamo. I don't wanna see your shrimp.
Back off, Ryota.
I'll send you to hell.

*Note: Takoyaki octopus dumplings are famous in Kansai.

The End!

*Note: Sort of like an energy bar.

POST SCRIPT

I felt like drawing a short manga for the first time in a while, and suddenly there were these two unfamiliar characters (nervous laugh), Tsuzuru Uesugi and Ryota Kamo from Kansai Division! Tsuzuru is the same age as Nanaki, 17 years old and a junior in high school, and Kamo is 21, a year older than Ao. Kamo is also a childhood friend of Ao. They met each other at a LOCK-affiliated school for psychics. Before they were assigned to separate divisions, they even briefly worked as partners. Tsuzuru is cruel, inhuman, has no sympathy for women and children, welcomes arguments, and is even more egotistical than Nanaki. He acknowledges and respects Ao's skills; however he always appears to argue with Nanaki (lol)! Kamo is the most decent (?) person in this group. He's always getting abused, but he keeps a positive, optimistic attitude. He loves gambling and dreams of making Tsuzuru crack up. ...Good luck (nervous laugh)! That's the story of our two guys from Kansai, but I have no plan for them to reappear after this. What in the world did I think them up for, then (nervous laugh)?! Finally, thank you for reading Nanaki. I'd like to give my thanks to my assistants for helping me with this manga; my editor, friends, acquaintances and family.

Thanks. See you again.

—Ryo Saenagi.

NEXT TIME IN

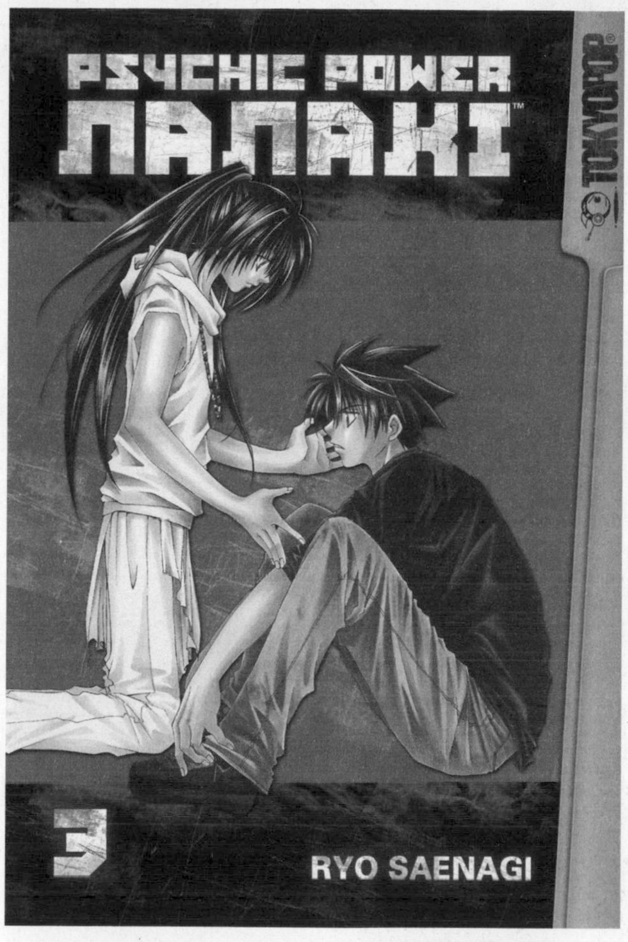

When a suspected vampire escapes from a mental institution, Nanaki and Ao are on the case again—except this time, they have to cooperate with the regular police! Are they doomed to become the vampire's next meal?